End of the Rainbow

Peter Quilter is recognized to be one of the most widely produced young playwrights in the world. His work has been produced in thirty-six countries and translated into twenty-three languages. His plays have been presented in major theatres in cities as diverse as Sydney, Amsterdam, Berlin, Johannesburg, Warsaw, Chicago, Caracas, Helsinki, Budapest, Rome, Montreal, Madrid, Rio de Janeiro and London.

He began his career in 1999 with the pop industry comedy *BoyBand* which played a summer season at the Gielgud Theatre in London's West End before travelling to Holland, Denmark, Poland, Slovakia, Estonia and South Africa. His work since then has ranged from female monologues (*Just the Ticket*) to farces (*Curtain Up*) musicals (*The Canterville Ghost*) and dramas (*Celebrity*).

In addition to the worldwide success of *End of the Rainbow*, Peter has also enjoyed international acclaim for his comedy *Glorious!* (*the True Story of Florence Foster Jenkins, the Worst Singer in the World*). The show played a six-month run at London's Duchess Theatre in 2006 starring Maureen Lipman and was nominated for the Olivier Award for Best New Comedy. *Glorious!* has since played in over a hundred theatres across six continents.

Peter is also the writer of the popular and award-winning 2009 comedy *Duets* – an evening comprised of four different plays, each performed in a tour de force by the same two actors. In 2011, he wrote two new plays – *The Nightingales* (a nostalgic musical based around a 1950s) and *The Morning After* (a mo in a bedroom).

Peter Quilter

End of the Rainbow

B L O O M S B U R Y

LONDON • NEW DELHI • NEW YORK • SYDNEY

Bloomsbury Methuen Drama

An imprint of Bloomsbury Publishing Plc

50 Bedford Square	1385 Broadway
London	New York
WC1B 3DP	NY 10018
UK	USA

www.bloomsbury.com

Bloomsbury is a registered trade mark of Bloomsbury Publishing Plc

First published in 2005 by Methuen Drama
Reprinted with revisions to the text 2012

Visit www.bloomsbury.com to find out more about our authors and their books
You will find extracts, author interviews, author events and you can sign up for
newsletters to be the first to hear about our latest releases and special offers.

British Library Cataloguing-in-Publication Data
A catalogue record for this book is available from the British Library.

ISBN: PB: 978-0-4137-7532-0
ePDF: 978-1-4081-5022-1
ePUB: 978-1-4081-5021-4

Library of Congress Cataloging-in-Publication Data
A catalog record for this book is available from the Library of Congress.

End of the Rainbow

To Felix
For everything

End of the Rainbow was first performed in this revised version in the UK at Royal & Derngate, Northampton on 5 February 2010, Artistic Director Laurie Sansom, Chief Executive Martin Sutherland, and received its first performance in the West End at Trafalgar Studios, London on 22 November 2010 presented by Lee Dean, Jenny Topper, Laurence Myers, Charles Diamond, Hilary Williams and David Bailey for Pinstripe Productions.

Judy Garland	Tracie Bennett
Anthony	Hilton McRae
Mickey Deans	Stephen Hagan
Radio Interviewer/Porter/ASM	Robin Browne

Director   Terry Johnson
Set and Costume Design   William Dudley
Lighting Design   Simon Corder
Sound Design   Gareth Owen
Musical Supervision   Gareth Valentine

The production received its North American premiere at the Guthrie Theater, Minneapolis on 28 January 2012, Artistic Director Joe Dowling. It featured the following cast and creatives:

Judy Garland	Tracie Bennett
Anthony	Michael Cumpsty
Mickey Deans	Tom Pelphrey
Radio Interviewer/Porter/ASM	Jay Russell

Director   Terry Johnson
Set and Costume Design   William Dudley
Lighting Design   Christopher Akerlind
Sound Design   Gareth Owen
Musical Supervision/
Musical Arrangements   Gareth Valentine
Orchestrations   Chris Egan
Musical Director/Conductor   Jeff Harris
Stage Manager   Mark Dobrow
Assistant Stage Manager   Rachel Zack

End of the Rainbow opened on Broadway at the Belasco Theatre on 2 April 2012, presented by Lee Dean, Laurence Myers, Joey Parnes, Ellis Goodman, Chase Mishkin, Shadowcatcher Entertainment/Alhadeff Productions, National Angels U.S. Inc., Charles Diamond/Jenny Topper, Myla Lerner/Barbara & Buddy Freitag, Spring Sirkin/Candy Gold, Hilary Williams and S.D. Wagner, John Johnson in association with the Guthrie Theater.

Judy Garland	Tracie Bennett
Anthony	Michael Cumpsty
Mickey Deans	Tom Pelphrey
Radio Interviewer/Porter/ASM	Jay Russell

Director   Terry Johnson
Set and Costume Design   William Dudley
Lighting Design   Christopher Akerlind
Sound Design   Gareth Owen
Orchestrations   Chris Egan
Musical Arrangements   Gareth Valentine
Music Direction   Jeffrey Saver
Music Coordinator   Seymour "Red" Press
Production Stage Manager   Mark Dobrow
Stage Manager   Rachel Zack

Characters

Judy Garland, *American, late forties, but looking much older*
Mickey Deans, *her American fiancé – early thirties*
Anthony, *her English pianist, fifties/sixties*
Radio Interviewer
Porter
ASM

It is Christmas 1968. A suite at the Ritz Hotel in central London.

Song List

'I Can't Give You Anything but Love' (Fields/McHugh)
'I Belong to London' (Anonymous)
'Just in Time' (Comden/Green/Styne)
'For Me and My Gal' (Goetz/Leslie/Meyer)
'You Made Me Love You' (Monaco/McCarthy)
'The Trolley Song' (Martin/Blane)
'The Man that Got Away' (Arlen/Gershwin)
'When You're Smiling' (Goodwin/Shay/Fisher)
'Come Rain or Come Shine' (Arlen/Mercer)
'Somewhere Over the Rainbow' (Arlen/Harburg)

Act One

Scene One

(Note: In this scene, although there are negative moments, the general feeling is optimistic and playful.)

A suite at the Ritz Hotel in London. A piano upstage centre. A stack of suitcases and a touring trunk. A pool of light reveals **Anthony** *at the piano. He plays a few bars of music – a gentle, quiet version of 'Somewhere Over the Rainbow'. He hears voices in the corridor (ad lib* **Judy** *and* **Mickey***) and stops playing. Wanting to surprise* **Judy***, he exits into the bathroom. The door opens and in walks* **Judy***, surveying the room. She switches on the lights.*

Judy It's smaller.

Enter **Mickey***, carrying a briefcase and an overnight bag.*

Mickey No, it isn't. They're all the same size.

Judy How would you know?

Mickey Because I asked.

Judy Then they lied to you. I've stayed here before. This room has shrunk

Mickey You remember the room? Half the time you don't know what city you're in.

Judy It's the little things I remember, not the big picture.

Mickey Let's not debate this.

Judy It's a room for midgets.

Mickey Can we change the subject?

Judy Oh, darling, that's fine. Change what you like, I can carry on by myself for hours.

Mickey Sure you can. But I know how to shut you up.

He grabs her and gives her a long kiss on the lips.

Judy   . . . Will you marry me?

Mickey   We already had that conversation.

Judy (*looking at her engagement ring*)   Oh yes, so we did.

Mickey   . . . You need to unpack.

Judy   Oh honey, I don't do that. I have people.

Mickey   Not any more you don't.

Judy   Oh. (*Looking at his groin.*) Well, then I think it might be time for *you* to unpack.

Mickey   Judy!

Judy   I just want to make sure nothing else in this hotel has shrunk.

*She gets on her knees and is undoing **Mickey**'s zipper when the bathroom door opens and **Anthony** steps out.*

Anthony   Hello!

Judy (*surprised*)   Anthony!

*Both are shocked. She gets to her feet and **Mickey** does up his zipper.*

Judy   . . . Is this *your* room?

Anthony   No, it's yours. I was in the bathroom.

Judy   You're sleeping in the bathroom? We have to pay you more.

Anthony   Please. They let me in to check the piano.

Judy   It's been for ever. I've missed you.

Anthony   Me too.

Judy   How long has it been?

Anthony   Last Christmas – in New York. Have you forgotten?

Judy   Of course not! You bought me that beautiful . . .

Anthony   Earrings.

Judy   That's right. I never take them off.

Anthony   But I haven't played for you for . . . Five years.
– Melbourne.

Judy   Melbourne?! Oh . . . I don't think Melbourne went
terribly well . . .

Anthony   No, it didn't.

Judy   But you're back to play for me anyway?

Anthony   Yes.

Judy   Good for you! Have you met my fiancé?

Anthony   We've spoken on the phone, that's all.

Judy   Well, now here he is in the flesh. (*Turning to* **Mickey**.)
The best thing that ever happened to me.

She pours herself into **Mickey**'s *arms for a fumbled loving embrace.*

She then turns back to **Anthony**.

Judy   Isn't he wonderful? And gorgeous?

Anthony (*changing subject referring to the cases*)   Travelling
light, are we?

Judy   The rest are in the lobby. Of course, half of them are
just stuffed with old towels, but you have to keep up
appearances.

Mickey   Judy, I need to go down and –

Judy   What?

Mickey   Give them some money.

Judy   No, Mickey, you stay here.

Mickey   I told you about this. You have to pay each week in
advance.

Judy   We'll see about that.

Mickey   Judy – let's not start a problem the first day we –

Judy   Mickey – angel – this is the kind of thing you have to leave to me. We'll pay them when it's convenient for us. Now what's the manager's name?

Mickey   Mr Crosby.

Judy   Fine. Leave Crosby to me.

Mickey   I just want everything to go smoothly.

Judy   Oh, it will. With you in charge! My God! This is going to be the biggest success of my career. And Top of the Town.

Anthony   Talk of the Town.

Judy   Correct! We're going bring it back from the dead. Just gimme six weeks. Mickey's a miracle worker, Anthony. He has got me everything I wanted. We have Delfont wrapped around our fingers. So – Mickey's in charge of *everything* from now on. He's going to be my full-time manager.

Mickey   I gave it all up – to be with Judy. But I'll continue with my business interests – keep the empire going.

Anthony   Yes. You run a club or something, don't you?

Mickey (*insulted*)   'Or something'? What does that mean?

Judy (*jumping in*)   It doesn't mean anything, darling. It's just the way he talks. – So! Here we all are! – In London. In the best hotel. In the smallest God damn suite they have . . .! . . . But at least they squeezed a piano in.

She goes over to the piano and looks around it.

. . . Is it in tune?

Anthony   Surprisingly – yes. First time ever, I think.

Mickey   That's because I arranged a tuner to come in this morning.

Judy   You did? – I told you – he's going to be the best manager in the world.

Mickey   I already am the best. They just don't know it yet.

Judy   You hear that? He takes right after me.

Anthony   How unfortunate . . .

A brief uncomfortable pause.

Judy   Ha! (*To* **Mickey**.) See – English humour. I warned you about that, right?

Mickey   Yeah.

Judy   They think irony is elegant, sarcastic sons of bitches. You have to behave yourself, Anthony. You're on board a tightly run ship. It's all been done. I've never known things worked out so far in advance. (*To* **Mickey**.) You're a wonder. You even got Anthony back.

Mickey   Well, that wasn't me – that was Delfont.

Judy   Even so! (*To* **Anthony**.) We've only been dating a couple of months. And look. (*She shows her engagement ring.*) Engaged after just one week. Isn't that amazing?

Anthony (*dryly*)   It's astonishing.

Judy   Husband number four.

Anthony   . . . Five.

Judy   What?

Anthony   It's five.

Judy   Is it? My God – who am I missing out? (*She thinks, then counts on her fingers.*) Grumpy, Dopey, Sleepy . . .

Anthony *laughs.*

Judy   Ha! I love it when you laugh. I can still make you laugh – that's good . . .?

Anthony   It's a miracle.

Judy   Well, yes. Because Melbourne . . . we had some problems, right?

Anthony   It was a bloodbath.

Judy   Yes. But here you are – and I'm thrilled. You're the best there is. Didn't I say that Mickey?

Mickey   Several times.

Judy   Oh, I'm just the luckiest woman alive. My favourite pianist. And – the love of my life.

She slobbers a kiss on **Mickey***'s lips, which seems as much for* **Anthony***'s benefit as anything else.*

Mickey   We should get these cases out of the way. You just relax.

Judy   Thank you, darling.

Anthony   Can I help?

Judy   Oh, please – you're so sweet.

She then goes over to the piano and plays a few keys as **Anthony** *and* **Mickey** *pick up various bags and cases and take them off into the bedroom, bathroom, etc.* **Mickey** *instinctively grabs the heavy trunk first and wheels it into a corner.* **Anthony***'s first choice is a tiny toiletry case which he delicately carries into the bathroom.* **Judy** *accompanies herself on piano to sing part of a song to* **Mickey***.*

Judy (*singing*)   'Just in time, I found you just in time . . .'

She looks over at **Mickey***, who smiles back and blows her a kiss. They continue with the cases.*

. . . Look at you two go! You're working like little –

Anthony   Munchkins?

Judy   I was going to say Mexicans. They're taller.

She plays the musical notes of 'Follow the Yellow Brick Road' on the piano and then grabs her own throat and chokes like she is being strangled. The cases are soon cleared and **Mickey** *and* **Anthony** *both take a seat.*

Judy   . . . Do you have any candy? I want something sweet.
Not a cigarette. They're very bad for you. Deanna Durbin
used to smoke all the time, even in school at the studio. She
was like a chimney. A chimney with one eyebrow that grew
all the way across.

Anthony *laughs, loving the Hollywood anecdotes.*

Judy   . . . Diana always sat next to Elizabeth Taylor. Oh! Liz
Taylor was *charming* . . . So charming you just wanted to run
her down with a car! Mickey Rooney smoked too – it stunts
your growth! . . . I liked school, but I never learned
anything. You should learn things. I lost so much time in
vaudeville. And we were a terrible act. We always followed
this comedian – *Happy* Harry. He was the saddest man I ever
met. Funny people just aren't funny. Don't you find that?
It's not a way to live. We all turned out very peculiar. Did I
get a cigarette? I asked for a cigarette.

Mickey *gives her a cigarette.*

Judy   Thank you . . . (*To* **Anthony**.) Where are you living
these days?

Anthony   Just down the corridor.

Judy   I mean – where are you living when we're not paying
for it?

Anthony   On the south coast – Brighton.

Judy   Oh. Is it nice there? Do they have fog?

Anthony   Not very often.

Judy   Are you sure?

She sits at the piano.

I love the fog.

Anthony   I'm sure.

Judy (*playing a couple of notes and then singing*)   'A foggy day
in . . . (*awkwardly*) Brighton town!' . . . No, you're right – no
fog.

She idly hits a few random piano keys.

. . . You know what I think? (*They don't answer.*) I think we should celebrate – and have a drink!

Mickey *and* **Anthony** *suddenly turn to look sternly at her.*

. . . What?!

Mickey   Judy –

Judy   What!? Just a drop of champagne or something. To mark the occasion.

Mickey   No!

Judy   Oh for Christ's sake. I'm not talking about passing out on the floor here. Just a half bottle of Dom Perignon – to make a toast.

Mickey   Not a drop.

Judy   Oh, Mickey.

Mickey   We've talked about this.

Judy   Yes, I know, but –

Mickey   You've got six weeks of concerts. That's not easy.

Judy   Now you listen to me –

Mickey (*tough*)   No. You listen to *me*! No booze, no pills, nothing. While we're here – I make the rules. So forget the champagne.

Judy   *Sid* would have let me.

Mickey   No he wouldn't! (*Testy.*) And who cares what 'Sid' would have done?

Judy   Sorry, darling, sorry. (*To* **Anthony**.) . . . He doesn't like it when I dig up the ex-husbands.

Mickey *shoots a look at* **Judy**.

Judy   . . . They don't get along.

Mickey   Judy!

Judy   I'm sorry, I'm sorry. Jesus.

Mickey   Well, it's always Sid and Vincent and what they –

Judy   Don't get testy – you're so testy. (*To* **Anthony**.) He gets spiky.

Mickey   I think anyone would get spiky if they had to keep hearing about –

Judy   I light candles. That's how *I* relax. I take a bath with lots of bubbles. Have you tried that darling?

Mickey   I'm fine, thank you.

Judy   Take a bath. Light some fucking candles.

Mickey   Is that what Sid used to do?

Judy   No. Though Vincent loved to bathe.

Mickey   You see – the ex-husbands again.

Judy   Well *you* brought them up!

Mickey *is about to carry on, but stops himself. Instead, he just laughs.* **Judy** *joins in the laughter.*

Judy (*after a moment*)   . . . So can I?

Mickey   No!

Judy   . . . Okay. You're in charge. (*A look to* **Anthony**.) . . . I'll tell you what – I'll get a couple of those hotel glasses that you use to clean your teeth. Fill them with water from the tap. Who needs Dom Perignon.

She flounces towards the bathroom.

Shut your eyes and we'll hardly notice the difference.

She exits.

Anthony   She hasn't changed.

Mickey   So they tell me.

Anthony   . . . What's the plan for today?

Mickey   I think we'll just go out and eat. Talk everything through – like, when you're gonna rehearse – and all that stuff.

Anthony   Fine.

Mickey   . . . I play too, you know.

Anthony   Play what?

Mickey   Piano. Jazz piano. I'm pretty good.

Anthony   Really? Well, that's a surprise.

Mickey   Yeah, that's me. I'm just full of surprises.

Anthony   (*gesturing to the piano*) Please – play something . . .

Mickey   I don't have to audition for you.

Anthony   Oh, I wasn't –

Mickey   Yes – yes, you were.

Judy *emerges with three glasses of water from the bathroom.*

Judy   Here we are! Now – let's do this.

The others reluctantly take a glass as she makes a toast.

To the show!

Mickey/Anthony   The show!

Judy   Judy's back!

Anthony   Again!

Judy   . . . Yes, again. But this time you better believe it . . . Oh – and to Mickey Deans. My husband to be. Who I love so much, I could just explode. Cheers, darling!

They toast their glasses and drink. **Mickey** *pulls a face immediately.* **Judy** *swills it all around her mouth, gargles, and then swallows.*

Judy   . . . It's not so bad. It's those Victorian pipes. (*A strain in her voice.*) Gives it a special twang.

The phone rings.

Anthony   I'll pour these down the sink.

*He collects the glasses, but **Judy** hangs on to hers. He heads back into the bathroom as **Mickey** answers the phone.*

Mickey   Hello? . . . Yeah, we're just heading out to eat, but you can leave the other cases in the room . . . Yes, Mr Crosby, I'll bring the money on the way down. (**Judy** *gets his attention.*) . . . Er – could you hang on? Miss Garland would like a word with you.

Judy *takes up the phone as **Anthony** returns. She puts on her best 'Judy Garland' voice.*

Judy   . . . Mr Crosby? Oh, I'm so pleased to speak to you in person. Now my darling fiancé is about to rush down to let you have some money, but would you mind if we dealt with this tomorrow? We've just arrived after a very tiring journey – and I do want to be at my best when you come to the opening night next week. You are coming I hope? . . . Oh, that's marvellous . . . Oh! That's very kind of you. I see we're going to become very good friends . . . yes . . . (*A forced chuckle.*) Oh yes . . . Goodbye.

She drops the performance immediately and puts the phone down.

Right – let's go eat.

Mickey   Ain't she something else.

Anthony   Oh, yes. Something else entirely.

Judy *strides over to the door.*

Judy (*to **Anthony***)   . . . Aren't you coming?

Anthony   I didn't know if I was invited.

Judy   Of course you're invited! . . . It's you that's paying.

She exits.

Mickey   She's not serious.

Anthony   Oh, I think she probably is.

As they both walk to the exit, fade to blackout. Music.

Scene Two

Lights rise on the hotel suite. The distant sound of traffic. The window is wide open and **Judy** *is sat perilously on the window ledge looking and leaning outwards.* **Anthony** *enters, not seeing her at first.*

Anthony   Hello . . . Hello?

Judy   Hello!

He is panicked and shocked when he suddenly sees her on the ledge.

But she remains calm – treating the entire episode as a bit of fun.

Anthony   Good God!

Judy   Hi.

Anthony   Get down.

Judy   Why?

Anthony   Judy!

Judy   I'm fine.

Anthony   Get down. (*Reaching to her.*) Take my hand.

Judy   No –

Anthony   Please! Judy!

Judy   Anthony – stop it! Pull yourself together! I am not going to jump!

The telephone rings.

Right – tell *him* that I'm jumping.

Anthony   What!?

Judy   Answer the phone – if it's Crosby, the manager, tell him I'm jumping – Anthony!

He moves to the phone and answers it.

Anthony (*into phone*)   . . . Yes? . . . Who is this?

Judy   Is it Crosby?

Anthony (*to* **Judy**)   Yes, it's Crosby.

Judy   Tell the son of a bitch I'm jumping!

Anthony (*into phone*)   She says she's jumping.

Judy   And – ?

Anthony   And you're a son of a bitch.

She screams. Then she silently mouths to him to hang up the phone. He does so.

Judy   Now he's crapping his pants. Bring the phone over.

He carries the phone over to the window.

Anthony   What's going on here?!

Judy   That low-life scumbag of a manager is threatening to throw me out.

Anthony   Why?

Judy   Because he's an asshole! . . . And we haven't paid the bill all week.

Anthony   But surely you can –

Judy   Relax. I'm handling it. If there's one thing I know, it's diplomacy.

The phone rings again. She answers it immediately.

(*Into the phone.*) You fucking cock sucker! Look at this mess you've got yourself into . . . How dare you threaten me! You wait for your God damn money like everybody else; what makes you so special? . . . No, it doesn't look good for my image, but right now I don't give one God damn what they write about me – and how's it gonna look for you and your pretty hotel when you got 'Dorothy' splattered all over your red carpet?! . . . And don't think I won't, because I'm so pissed with this place that I might just do anything . . .Yes, I hope we can!

She slams down the telephone.

(*To* **Anthony**.) We're going to come to 'an arrangement'.

Anthony   Are you getting down now?

Judy   In a minute. I kinda like it.

Anthony   Please . . .

Judy   Come here.

He moves very close to her.

Judy   Look at them all. Like little ants, craning their necks, all excited. You think they want me to jump? Is that what they're waiting for? Give them something to talk about when they get home.

Anthony   I think they already have that.

He offers his hand to her. And she begins to climb off the ledge.

But first she gives the crowd a wave and we hear distant whistles, cheers and applause. She then moves away from the window. She reveals that she has a glass of vodka and grapefruit to hand. She takes a sip.

Judy   What are you doing here anyway?

Anthony   We had a rehearsal.

Judy   We did?

Anthony   Yes.

Judy   Well nobody told me. You still want to do it?

Anthony   I think, in the circumstances –

Judy   Oh hell to the circumstances! We still got the room, don't we? And I'm not spread across the sidewalk, so – life goes on.

Anthony   Pavement.

Judy   Huh?

Anthony   We call it a pavement here, not a sidewalk.

Judy   Oh, do we now?

Anthony   We do.

Judy   Good – glad we got that cleared up. Now play the fucking piano.

Anthony   Do you think we could curb the swearing a little this afternoon? I'm a bit on edge – I don't like that kind of thing.

Judy   Crap. I'm going to tell the papers you 'saved my life'.

He smiles.

Judy   You like that? That would be wild, wouldn't it. You'd become an icon. The 'queens' would worship you.

Anthony   They already do . . .

He makes his way to the piano.

Judy   You'll never touch me. To them, I'm a goddess. I could vomit my dinner in their laps and I'd still be glamorous.

Anthony   What a charming picture – thank you.

He is by now sat at the piano. He plays a lengthy arpeggio introduction and waits for her to sing – which she doesn't.

Anthony   Whenever you're ready . . .?

Judy   Let me warm up first.

She lights up a cigarette and takes a puff. Then signals she's ready.

Anthony   Let's just mark it through. See if it's still there.

Judy   It may be – I might not.

Anthony *repeats a brief arpeggio.* **Judy** *begins to sing.*

SONG
'I CAN'T GIVE YOU ANYTHING BUT LOVE'

She has sung only the first half dozen lines of the song when suddenly the door opens and **Mickey** *enters, interrupting.*

Mickey   Can someone please explain to me what the hell is going on?!

Judy   Nothing much.

Mickey   Nothing m— . . . You threatened to jump out the window!

Judy   Negotiations, that's all.

Anthony   There was a problem with the bill.

Judy   Shut up.

Mickey   I thought we'd paid the bill.

Judy   So did I.

Mickey   Judy – there's twenty press in the lobby. And the BBC.

Judy   Good! Some publicity at last.

Mickey   What do I tell them?

Judy   That I was driven to despair by the size of this fucking hotel room.

Mickey   It's the same size as all the others.

Judy   Oh, don't start on that one again. You think I don't know the difference?

Mickey   It doesn't matter. I don't want to argue about that now.

Judy   You think *I* want to argue? I don't want to argue.

Mickey   You always want to argue – it's like you can't survive without –

Judy   That is not true, that is not –

Mickey   It's like fucking Ritalin for you.

Judy   You're the one that argues.

Mickey   Me?

Judy   Oh yes – always rattling along over some stupid thing or other.

Mickey   I don't believe this –

The following speeches take place simultaneously as they try to talk over each other. Near the beginning of these speeches, **Anthony** *starts to accompany the argument on piano, playing Mozart's Sonata in C.*

Judy   One fucking tirade or another. I just want an easy life, but you – oh God, you have to argue about everything . . .You lay awake at night conjuring up new ideas for some verbal torture you can throw at me with that huge mouth that you carry around like fucking luggage . . . I don't want to argue all the time, I just want a bit of peace and understanding. But I never get it and I've had it, you hear?

Mickey   I never argued with anybody until you came along – you're like some kind of fucking demon . . . You don't listen, you just shout and shout for hours without saying anything at all and it's exhausting. Christ – it wears me out . . . Can't you just switch off and actually listen to someone? It's a nightmare – you go on and on and on . . . How am I supposed to live with that? I just never get a fucking break.

Judy   Stop it! Stop it!

Anthony *stops playing piano and* **Mickey** *stops arguing.*

Judy   I don't want to do this anymore! We're trying to rehearse!

Mickey   Fine! I'll handle it – I'll say it was food poisoning, made you light-headed or something – just don't you speak to anybody – alright? And don't leave here for the rest of the day.

Judy   I'm starving!

Mickey   Room service.

Judy   Not on your life.

Mickey (*reluctantly giving in*)   . . . What do you want?

Judy   . . . Roast beef.

Mickey   Roast – ? I don't know where to get that.

Judy   Just drive around until you smell gravy . . .

Mickey *sucks it up and heads for the exit.*

Judy   . . . Isn't he handsome when he's angry. (*Shouting after* **Mickey**.) . . . With horseradish!

Mickey *exits, slamming the door behind him.*

Anthony   Shall we get on?

Judy   With what?

He hands a song from his folder to her.

Anthony   Let's try the new opener.

She puts her cigarette out. He starts to play the tacky song introduction.

Judy   . . . You're kidding me right?

Anthony   I'm only playing what's written

SONG
'I BELONG TO LONDON'

Judy (*singing*)   I belong to London . . .

(*Spoken.*) . . . I'll leave this lyric out, they'll be applauding . . .

She crosses the line out with a pencil and then continues to sing from the third line of the song. When reaching the word 'home' in the lyric, she avoids singing this top note, but instead points a finger upwards.

Anthony   Coward!

She then sings the final line of the song. The piano plays out.

She starts to cough a little. He fetches her a glass of water.

Judy   . . . What a shitty song . . .!

He hands her the water.

Anthony   Here.

Judy   Thank you.

Anthony   Always a pleasure, never a chore.

Judy   Oh, you're all so polite here, I love it. (*She drinks and then stares blankly at the glass.*) Whenever I drink water I always feel I'm missing out on something . . . There has to be a tablet somewhere I could take.

Anthony   There's nothing here.

Judy   Don't I know it.

Anthony   It's great that you're managing without.

Judy   It's not easy. Especially when I know there's a doctor a block away ready to provide me with anything I want.

Anthony   Without a prescription?

Judy   Sometimes even without an autograph . . . I've been doing this for over thirty years, there isn't a trick I can't pull. Back in LA I had pills sewn into the hems of dresses, taped to the back of furniture. It wasn't the police who raided me, it was the family. And they're worse. When your sister-in-law finds a bottle of Benzedrine hidden in your panties, you don't even have rights to an attorney.

Anthony   Maybe she was just trying to help you.

Judy   I didn't need help – I needed pills. No one ever got a grip of that. Least of all Minnelli. And Sid didn't know the half of it.

Anthony   Do you miss – any of them?

Judy   No. But I miss . . . being loved.

Anthony   I didn't think there *was* anyone more loved than you.

Judy   That's not the same, Anthony – and you know it. But that's all changed. I have Mickey now.

Anthony   Yes, and at such speed. We should phone the *Guinness Book of Records*.

Judy   Oh listen to you, you cynic. Don't you believe in love at first sight?

Anthony   Well . . . I do – (**Anthony** *sings*.) . . . 'but not for me'.

He plays a run of notes and she carries on with the first song, 'I Can't Give You Anything but Love'. She sings another four lines of the song before she interrupts herself –

Judy   So who are you bringing to the opening night?

Anthony   I don't know.

Judy   What about your parents?

Anthony   They live in Inverness.

Judy   So take a cab.

Anthony   It's in Scotland.

Judy   You should take me to Scotland. You can present me as your new girlfriend.

Anthony   Oh, I couldn't do that. They've suffered enough . . .

Judy   Well, thank you!

Anthony   What I mean is, they're confused enough already. I don't want to give them false hope.

Judy   Well then, we'll just say we met at Alcoholics Anonymous.

Anthony   That would be much better.

Judy   Why Scotland anyway? What the hell are they doing there?

Anthony   Furthest they could get from me on this island without drowning . . . Key change.

He plays a chord – and waits. She sings the final lines of the song, but he cuts in after the final 'but'. He calls out, cuing the band –

Anthony   Five, six, seven, eight!

His call cues a transition into a concert sequence. The band immediately strikes up, playing an energetic repeat of the previous bars of the song and they are revealed on stage for the first time – ideally in a coup de théâtre where the reveal is a surprise for the audience, the band previously having been completely hidden behind a flat or gauze. There is a lighting change at the same time as the music starts. **Judy** *exits for a quick costume change, at the very least putting on a jacket if a full change is not possible, and she takes up a microphone. The setting transforms simply to the stage of the Talk of the Town. On cue with the music, she re-enters and repeats the final lines of the song in concert mode.*

The band concludes the song with her and she bows to the audience. Applause. Then segue into the next song –

SONG
'JUST IN TIME'

After the first section of the song, she breaks to talk to the audience, the band continuing softly underneath.

Judy   Ladies and gentlemen, I would like to take a moment to introduce you to someone very special. A man who I simply adore. Who fills my heart with a greater love than I have ever known. He's my fiancé, my manager and my protector – Mickey Deans. Come on out here, my darling. (*To the audience, encouraging them to applaud.*) Mickey Deans everyone! Mickey Deans!

Mickey *joins her on stage – at first, somewhat taken aback and embarassed.*

They kiss. Polite applause is heard.

Judy   This is dedicated to you, my angel.

She continues the song, now at full throttle, playing the next part of it to **Mickey** *– and he begins to relish the attention. But shortly, her* *attention turns back completely to the audience and he exits, a little awkwardly. She concludes the song and the music plays out. Blackout.*

Scene Three

We return to the hotel room. Some days later. **Mickey** *is on the couch, reading the newspapers.* **Judy** *is in the bathroom.*

Judy *(from within the bathroom)* Oh, my God – they've made me look like the Bride of Frankenstein. I have never worn a head scarf like that in my entire life. They've pasted it on. And they've aged me. There has to be some law. Mickey, there has to be a law –

Mickey I'm trying to read this.

Judy Look at the picture first. If I look like I've been dead twenty years, don't read the text. It'll be fiction, like the photograph. You listening to me?

Mickey Do I have a choice?

Judy What does it say?

Mickey They like you.

Judy What picture?

Mickey On the stage – with your hand sticking out.

Judy *(horrified)* Oh – sounds wonderful! . . . How old do I look?

Mickey Erm . . . I'd say . . .

Judy What?

Mickey . . . A hundred and . . .

Judy Oh, shut up.

The bathroom door flies open and she bursts into the room. She flings a couple of newspapers across the room as she enters.

I don't want to read any more. It's all the same garbage.

Mickey   At least they're talking about you.

Judy   They're not talking Mickey, they're reviewing. They weren't supposed to be doing that till next week.

Mickey   What's the difference?

Judy   It was a 'preview'. We were still trying things out. You don't invite press to a preview, you invite them to the 'press night' – that's how it got the name! What shoes am I wearing?

Mickey   Whichever. It doesn't matter.

Judy   It *does* matter. The blue ones are too tight, the black ones are too dull and I'm not wearing Chanel on the radio.

Mickey   So pick another pair.

Judy   I don't have time for that.

Mickey   I'm not your dresser.

Judy   Fine – I'll go in my bare feet. You shit bag.

Mickey   Hey – shut up, pull yourself together, and pick out some fucking shoes.

Judy   I don't wanna pick out the shoes!

Mickey   Stop yelling – it's not important what shoes you wear.

Judy   Not to you – you always look like crap.

Mickey   . . . Wear the brown ones.

Judy   What brown ones?

Mickey   The brown ones.

Judy   I have *brown* ones?

Mickey   I bought you some brown ones.

Judy   Oh those . . . I gave those to the maid. (**Mickey** *gives her a look.*) . . . Even she hated them.

Mickey   Judy – I don't care. Life is too short to get into this.

Judy   Keep talking to me like that and life's gonna get even shorter.

She grabs a pair of red shoes.

. . . I'll wear the red ones.

She sits down and proceeds to put on the red shoes.

Mickey   Great idea. Click the heels together and you'll get there even quicker . . .!

He laughs out loud, thoroughly amused by his own joke. She just glares at him, as though ready to kill him.

Judy   . . . Fuck-head!

He goes back to reading the paper.

. . . What time is it? (*No answer.*) Mickey! What time –

Mickey   Eleven.

Judy   . . . So when have we got to be there?

Mickey   They're sending a car for twelve.

Judy   This radio guy, what's he like?

Mickey   I don't know – regular guy, what do you mean?

Judy   Is he famous here?

Mickey   I think he's well known.

Judy   *I mean* – what's he gonna do, piss on me, or kiss my ass?

Mickey   They don't seem to go for either on the radio in England. They just seem to sail down the middle. Not offend anyone. It's all just pleasant and cosy.

Judy   Sounds hideous.

Mickey   Hey – I set this up, remember. Me. I made a special effort, so I'd appreciate it if you'd –

Judy   Oh, stop it, stop it. You make one phone call and expect a round of applause.

Mickey   I don't want applause, I just – Just appreciate that it's not that easy.

Judy   To get on the radio? Have you listened to the people they put on the air here? . . . And tell them I won't sing. They always ask me to sing something. A royal command performance for some grey old radio hack. I won't do it. It pisses me off!

Mickey   Christ, what is your problem?

Judy   Don't question me.

Mickey   If you want me to be your manager, then I need to know what's going on in your head. I've got a reputation to think of too. I don't want you sitting there, live on the BBC, suddenly flying off the handle.

Judy   And when have I ever done that? . . . On the radio? When?

Mickey   There's always a first time.

Judy   I'm a professional. Down to the soles of my shitty brown shoes.

Mickey   There you go again.

Judy   I'm just nervous, damn it.

Mickey   Well, you have to get over that.

Judy   I have to get over a lot of things. You can either help me or sneer at me.

He sneers. He perhaps even dismissively peels himself a banana and takes a bite. In response, she goes over to the piano and takes out a very well-hidden bottle of pills. She gives them a shake loud enough for him to hear.

Mickey   What are those?

Judy   Grown-up candy.

Mickey   Judy – !

Judy   They're just tablets, Mickey. I can take a couple of tablets.

He stands and approaches her.

Mickey   Not while I'm in charge. Give them to me.

Judy   No.

Mickey   Don't make me take them by force.

Judy   You wouldn't dare!

Mickey (*tough, scary*)   Wouldn't I?!

She looks in his eyes and realises that he would. She hands him the bottle of pills. He reads the label.

. . . Who is Doctor Yang?

Judy   . . . A Chinaman.

Mickey   I could have guessed that. Is he in London?

Judy   He brought his lovely Mrs Yang to the show last night and I asked him for a small favour, and he dropped them off later. I know what I'm doing, they're mild.

Mickey   No, they're not.

Judy   And what would you know? You get high on aspirin.

Mickey   I know plenty . . . I'm keeping these.

Judy   The hell you are.

*They begin a physical struggle as she tries to get the pills back. The tussle becomes an evocative mix of physical battle and sexual foreplay. Half a fight over the pills, half an erotic manhandling of each other. She fails to get hold of the pills, even though she got hold of almost everything else. The door opens. **Anthony** enters, carrying* *a pile of dirty bed sheets, which he dumps just inside the door. He watches the erotic struggle for a moment.*

Anthony   . . . Is this a bad time?

Judy *removes herself from the fight.*

Judy   Anthony, get my pills back for me. Mickey has stolen them.

Anthony   Pills?

Mickey   She was about to take Ritalin.

Anthony   I don't understand, you were doing so well.

Judy   They're nothing. They're mild. What is the matter with you people? (*Spotting the pile of bed sheets.*) And what the hell are those bed sheets doing back here?

Anthony   They were outside the door.

Judy   Put them back out, They've not been cleaned.

Anthony   They won't take them. I've already asked.

Mickey   Why?

Anthony   Because of the unpaid bills. They're not doing our laundry anymore.

Mickey   Christ. Judy, you have to pay them.

Judy   The hell I do.

Mickey   Let me at least give them something, just to get them off our back.

Judy   I don't have anything. How much are we getting for the radio interview?

Mickey   That's minimal, a small fee.

Judy   Will it cover my bed sheets?

Mickey   Of course it will, but –

Judy   So send them to the Ying Yang Laundry! Screw Crosby and his hotel Nazis.

Anthony   Look – *I'll* pay for the laundry and I'll take care of the Ritalin. Okay? I think that's the best thing.

Mickey   No, I think it's the best thing that I keep them. She'll only talk you into giving them back.

Anthony   I won't let her.

Mickey   I'm not taking that chance.

Anthony   Well, then hide them or bin them or –

Judy   Oh, just give me the pills! You guys are so naive. You think I can't get tablets any time I want? Day or night? I've got address books filled with chink quacks and dyke doctors who'll fall over themselves to help me out. I've been stepping around guys like you for years. (*To* **Mickey**.) Sid was just like you – got very fidgety. He didn't like the pills. But at least he wasn't a hypocrite.

Mickey   Meaning?

Judy   Meaning – Mickey – who the hell was it *providing* me with drugs just six weeks ago?

Mickey   That was before I really knew you.

Judy   So?

Mickey   I was helping you out. You were a guest in the club, that's what we do.

Judy   Oh – you were providing a service?

Mickey   Kind of, yes.

Judy   Well, I tell you, the service has really gone down hill!

Mickey   I didn't realise then, what a . . . I didn't know how . . . What I mean is –

Judy   – Oh Christ, finish the sentence before I kill myself.

Mickey   I made a mistake. Okay? You get used to just giving people what they want without thinking – drink, hookers, drugs – that's the way clubs are.

Judy   Fine. Let's go to a club, then you can force-feed me the damn things.

Mickey   No.

Judy   Stop saying 'no' to me!

Mickey   You'll never get clear of them if you keep –

Judy (*yelling*)   I don't want to get clear! – because I don't *need* to get clear. Just a little bit of help to sleep and a little bit of help to sing. That's no crime.

Anthony   Judy, I agree with Mickey. You have to –

Judy   Oh – God!

She flings a random object across the room.

Let me explain something to you fellas. I have swallowed and vomited more drugs than you could possibly imagine. What I'm taking now is nothing – nothing – to what I was taking at home. Amphetamines, narcotics, uppers, downers, cocktails of Benzedrine and Dexedrine, all washed down with alcohol. Seconal, Tuinal, tranquilisers, energisers, and – Ritalin! I was buzzing! You could have shoved cables into me and powered Manhattan! . . . And where am I at the end of it all? Still standing. Centre stage, boys. Centre stage.

Anthony   But for how long?

Judy (*to* **Anthony**, *vicious*)   As long as they want me!

Anthony *avoids further confrontation and quietly exits.*

Judy   (*to* **Mickey**, *more calmly*)   . . . You're a sweet man. And I love that you care for me. That you're my protector. But you need to let me look after myself sometimes. That's my right.

She puts her hand out. He does nothing.

Judy   . . . I ruined my life once. I'm not about to do it
again. I need those. And without them, I'm not leaving this
room, or going to the radio, or doing the show. Because
without them, I can't do these things. I need a little bit of
help. But I heard what you said. Really I did. And Judy's
gonna be a good girl.

She starts to gently sing to him.

You made me love you . . . I didn't wanna do it . . . I didn't
wanna do it . . .

He slowly relents and shakes one single tablet out of the bottle.

Mickey   Just one.

Judy   Just one . . .

She smiles and gently takes the pill from his hand. She sings again.

. . . You know you made me love you . . .

She puts the pill in her mouth.

Fade to blackout.

Scene Four

*A piece of music plays as a link into the next sequence. A pool of light
rises on* **Judy** *and a BBC* **Radio Interviewer** *who wears a
colourful sweater. They are live on the radio.*

Radio Interviewer   It's such a pleasure to welcome to the
BBC the legendary Judy Garland – and I must say, you
look delightful.

Judy   Oh, thank you.

Radio Interviewer   Judy – may I begin by asking – we're
always reading of your private life in the papers – often very
dramatic stories. How much of this should we believe?

Judy Oh, all of it, darling, all of it! (*Laughs.*) Otherwise, it's just no fun. If you knew how dull and ordinary my life was in reality, you would all be so bored.

Radio Interviewer You don't mind all the stories?

Judy Hell, no. What we do is – I mean, the two of us, what we . . . I'm sorry, I forgot the question.

Radio Interviewer The stories in the –

Judy Oh yes, yes. I sit up with Mickey in the evenings and we read it all and laugh like drains. (*She laughs.*)

Radio Interviewer Your speaking, of course, of your current 'beau' – Mickey Deans.

Judy You know – I'll tell you what's the reason I'm distracted. It's the top you're wearing. It's kaleidoscopic.

Radio Interviewer Well, our listeners will have to take your word for that.

Judy Yes they will! Is your sex life as colourful as your sweater?!

He lets out an embarassed laugh, then rapidly changes subject.

Radio Interviewer Let's talk now about your concert at the Talk of the Town. Six whole weeks.

Judy I think they're seeing how many shows I can do before I fall over. Are you coming to see me Brian?

Radio Interviewer I am indeed. Although my name is Donald.

Judy Oh! . . . As in the Duck?

Radio Interviewer I suppose so . . .

Judy I'm sorry – that was very rude. I'm not quite myself today. Please forgive me. You must come and have dinner with me and my fiancé after the show one night. Okay? We'll go out, the three of us – Mickey, Donald and – (*referring to herself*) Goofy!

They both chuckle at this.

Radio Interviewer   I would love to.

Judy   Good . . . Love to what?

Radio Interviewer   . . . You invited me to dinner.

Judy   Did I really? I'm always doing that. I'll invite anybody! (*Judy realises the interviewer is offended but soldiers on*) . . . One day they'll all turn up and it'll be terrible – just terrible. It's really all – . . . I'm sorry, this isn't going very well.

Radio Interviewer   No, no, it's absolutely – . . . I expect you're focused on your concert tonight.

Judy   I have a concert tonight? Oh yes – I suppose I must have. Though how on earth they expect me to – . . . Does this place have a liquor cabinet? I mean, my God, how you all survive on *tea* I will never – (*She gives up.*) . . . Can I go now?

Radio Interviewer   . . . Well, of course – You must be a very busy lady.

Judy   You can just put on a record, right?

Radio Interviewer   Yes, that's the easy bit. Ladies and gentlemen – Miss Judy Garland!

Music kicks in immediately. Blackout and we move sharply into a concert sequence. The band is revealed again. This is **Judy** *singing at her best, on excellent form –*

SONG MEDLEY
'FOR ME AND MY GAL'
'YOU MADE ME LOVE YOU.'
'THE TROLLEY SONG'

At the end of the routine – blackout.

Scene Five

The hotel suite, later that night. **Mickey** *is on the telephone.*
Anthony *is checking under the piano, looking for hidden pills.*

Mickey (*on the phone*)   . . . Well, I'd rather you checked. It's
a favourite place of hers so she's as likely to be there as
anywhere else . . . yes, check again. This is important. You
have my number? . . . Thank you.

He puts the phone down and turns to **Anthony**.

Mickey   Did you check the bathroom?

Anthony   Twice.

Mickey   What about the tank?

Anthony   There's nothing. Look, I'd prefer not to be
doing this.

Mickey   I can't help that. (*He dials a new number.*) I'm calling
The Ivy.

Anthony   I'd like to go to my room.

Mickey   Don't be stupid. We have a crisis here.

Anthony   We don't have a crisis. She did a great show and
just went out to celebrate.

Mickey   She never just 'goes out'. And don't tell me I can't
recognise a crisis, because I can. (*His phone call is answered.*)
. . . Yes, I need to speak to the restaurant manager . . . It's
Mickey Deans . . . Mickey *Deans* . . . Judy Garland's fiancé
. . . (*This time it works.*) . . . Thank you. (*To* **Anthony**.) Could
you keep looking?

Anthony   I've looked everywhere.

Mickey (*into the phone*)   . . . Yes, hi. – Is Judy Garland there
tonight? . . . Well, I need you to break your policy and tell
me, because we have an emergency here . . . She isn't? Then
why the big charade you asshole?!

He slams the phone down.

Anthony   I guess we won't be eating there again.

Mickey   I can't think of anywhere else. Jesus! . . . What about your queer friends, can't we call them?

Anthony   None of them were watching the show tonight – and I resent you calling my friends –

Mickey (*dismissing the sentence*)   Oh, shut up.

Anthony   Fine. Goodnight, Mickey.

He heads for the door.

Mickey   No, no – come on, I need help here.

Anthony   I don't give a monkey's.

Mickey   If she comes in drunk, it's gonna take both of us.

Anthony   I was hired as a pianist.

Mickey   You were hired as Judy Garland's pianist. That's a wider job description.

Anthony   . . . You know, saying 'please' might help a little.

Mickey   Okay – 'Please' . . . Please! . . . What? You want me to buy you chocolates as well?

Anthony   No, but I'd at least like a drink.

Mickey   Fine. Whisky?

Anthony   Soda water.

Mickey   Oh right – the hard stuff.

Mickey *pours out a glass of whisky for himself and a soda water.* **Anthony** *sits.*

Mickey   . . . I can't believe she gave me the slip. She had the stage door guy distract me.

Anthony   The blond? Yes, he distracts me too . . .!

Mickey *brings over the drinks,* **Anthony** *takes his.*

Anthony Cheers.

Mickey (*pointed*) . . . Bottoms up!

Anthony *gives* **Mickey** *a weary smile and they both drink. Nothing said for a moment.* **Mickey** *sits also.*

Mickey . . . Are you single?

Anthony (*mock surprise*) I'm sorry?

Mickey It's a question, not a proposal.

Anthony Oh. Well, in that case – Yes. For about six months now. I broke up with someone over the summer.

Mickey Who was he?

Anthony His name was Nigel. He was Australian, a dancer. We were together for quite some time . . . and then he went.

Mickey (*drily*) Suicide?

Anthony No. He just moved on . . . To a woman, in fact.

Mickey (*smiling, intrigued*) Really?

Anthony Yes, I thought you'd like that.

Mickey A woman. Wow . . . You drove him straight . . .!

He has a good laugh over this.

Anthony I'm so pleased to have amused you. You're such a confidence booster – they should hire you out.

Mickey Well, be fair. You have to admit it's funny.

Anthony Actually, no. It was extremely un-funny. I liked him a lot.

A brief pause. They drink.

. . . And what about you? Turned any women lesbian this month?

Mickey . . . Not this month.

The phone rings. **Mickey** *grabs it.*

Mickey   Yes? . . . Right, okay. (*Puts the phone down.*) She's on her way up.

Anthony   How is she?

Mickey   The porter's *carrying* her.

We hear **Judy** *from the corridor.*

Judy (*offstage*)   Hey – put me down . . . I said – put me down, you idiot!

The hotel **Porter** *walks into the room, carrying* **Judy** *in his arms. She looks wretched. There is a large graze on her forehead, red and bloodied.* **Anthony** *rushes forward.*

Anthony   Oh my God, your head! What happened?

Judy   What are you asking me for? How the hell would I know! (*To the* **Porter**.) Put me down!

(*To the others.*) I think he's hanging on to me till he gets a tip.

Anthony *grabs some coins from his pocket and gives them to the* **Porter**, *who unceremoniously dumps* **Judy** *down onto the sofa.*

Anthony   Thank you. I'll get something for that graze.

He goes back into the bathroom as the **Porter** *exits.*

Mickey   Where the hell have you been?

Judy   Don't you raise your voice to me!

Mickey   I wasn't!

Judy   I know, I'm just warning you not to! I'm entitled to go out on my own sometimes, you know. I am a card-carrying adult – alright!

Mickey   You're drunk as hell.

Judy   That's right. And I love it. You should try it too, Mickey. People might like you more.

Mickey   Oh, why don't you fuck off.

Judy   Hey – I'm Judy Garland – you show me some respect!

Mickey   And I'm your fiancé. So why don't you start to fucking earn it!

She grabs the bowl of fruit and hurls it across the room at him. It misses him and smashes against the wall, the fruit flying everywhere. **Anthony** *enters, managing to avoid the tumbling fruit.*

Anthony   I found some antiseptic.

Mickey   When you're done, hide it, or she'll try and drink it.

Judy   Oh – suck my dick!

Anthony   Judy – I need to bathe that wound.

Judy   What?

Anthony   You have a nasty graze on your forehead.

She feels her forehead and then checks her fingers for blood.

Judy   Where is it?

Anthony   Just stay still for a second.

He wets a handkerchief with the antiseptic and attempts to dab it on the graze.

Mickey   How did you get the cut? Fall over in front of a bunch of photographers? Can we expect to see it in the papers tomorrow?

Judy (*to* **Anthony**)   Is there a way that we can get him to just leave?

Mickey   Answer the question! I need to know if I have to invent another story.

Judy   No, you don't. I just tripped or something. Or some guy pushed me – I just forget. Who gives a damn, anyway. There were no photos, alright?

Mickey   Good. Because I've never seen you look so ugly!

She lunges at **Mickey** *again, but* **Anthony** *holds her back.*

Anthony   Mickey, would you shut up! That isn't helping. Judy, please – just stay still.

She gets to her feet and approaches **Mickey**, *confrontational.*

Judy (*to* **Mickey**)   You bastard son of a bitch!

Anthony   He doesn't mean any of it – you've just made him angry.

Judy (*still at* **Mickey**)   You homo!

Anthony *calmly goes over to her and takes her by the hand to lead her back to the sofa.*

Anthony   No, dear, I'm the homo . . .

They sit again on the sofa.

. . . and we've been sat here worrying about you for hours.

Judy   You don't need to worry – I can handle myself.

Anthony   Yes, that's already apparent.

He continues to bathe the wound.

Judy (*to* **Anthony**)   You're hurting me.

Anthony   I'm trying to stop it getting infected.

Judy (*impatient*)   Oh, just leave it.

Anthony   In a second.

Judy   I said – leave it! (*She brushes* **Anthony** *away and stands up.*) . . . I need a drink.

Mickey   No, you don't. You're not having anything.

Judy   Don't you try and control me, Mickey. I make the decisions.

Mickey   We'll see about that.

Judy   Yes – we *will* see.

Mickey   The last time you ran your own life, look what happened.

Judy   Take a look at *your* own life – you think you did so great?

Mickey   I hate it when you're like this.

Judy   Like what? – Where's my drink?

Mickey   You're not getting a drink. I'll order some coffee.

Judy   Screw the coffee!

She hunts around the room for the liquor bottles.

Where is it?

Mickey   It's gone, so forget it.

Judy   Where's the whisky?

Mickey   Start straightening yourself out – you've got a show tomorrow.

Judy (*laughing at this suggestion*)   Ha! – I'm *not* doing a show tomorrow.

Mickey   Yes you are.

Judy   Now you listen to me. I decide if and when I do shows. And I am not doing one tomorrow –

Mickey   Yes you are.

Judy   So you can get on the phone and start giving back the tickets.

Mickey   That's not gonna happen.

Judy   Are you listening to me? No show! I took the roof off of that place tonight. I gave them everything I have. And now we're gonna get the hell out of here because I just can't do that again. There's nothing left. Cancel the show.

Mickey   And then want? We walk away from here with *nothing*? (*He goes right up to her.*) We agreed at the start of all this I would be the guy who looks after you. That's what you wanted – and that's exactly what I'm doing. So tonight you can rant and rave as much as you like. But when the sun comes up tomorrow you are getting ready for a show, regular as clockwork.

Judy   Is that your final word?

Mickey   Yes.

Judy   Well here are *my* final words –

She grabs a nearby cushion and whacks him hard with it on each word.

(*Yelling.*) I – don't – want – to!

She turns from him, throws the cushion to the floor, and storms into the toilet. On her way, she notices **Anthony**'s *bag on a nearby chair and takes it in there with her. Neither* **Anthony** *or* **Mickey** *see her grabbing the bag.*

Anthony (*very dry*)   . . . I thought that went very well . . .

Mickey   It was fine. I had the whole thing under control.

Anthony   You did . . .?! Somehow I missed that.

Mickey   This is how she tests me. If I let her beat me down, I'll never get my way again. I know that woman really well.

Anthony   You've only known her ten minutes.

Mickey   She's not that complicated.

Anthony   Well . . . far be it from me to argue with her husband to be . . .

Mickey   That's right.

Anthony   Are you sure she'll go on tomorrow?

Mickey   She'll go on. I've seen her worse than this.

Anthony   Really?! That must have been fun!

He heads for the door.

Mickey   You're not going?

Anthony   Yes, I'm going. I'm definitely going, so let's not even discuss it. I'll order some coffee for her from my room. (*Looking for his bag.*) . . . Where is it?

Mickey   What?

Anthony   My bag was here.

Mickey *realises* **Judy** *must have taken the bag into the bathroom with her.*

Mickey   . . . Was there anything in it? Anything she'd like?

Anthony   No, of course not.

Mickey *bangs on the bathroom door.*

Mickey   Have you got Anthony's bag? (*Bangs again.*) You hear me?

The door flies open, **Judy** *exiting. She throws the bag to* **Anthony**.

Judy   I hear you.

She crosses to the sofa as **Anthony** *checks through his bag.*

Anthony   . . . Oh God!

Mickey   What?

Anthony   She's taken these.

He holds up an empty pill bottle.

Mickey   What are they?

Anthony   They're for my sister's cocker spaniel . . . He has mange.

Judy   Oops!

She throws herself on the sofa.

Mickey   Call a doctor.

Judy   Screw the doctor. I don't need a doctor.

Mickey   They're for a fucking spaniel!

Judy   Then call a fucking vet! . . . (*She raises her leg.*) If I piss up a lamp post, *then* you call a doctor.

Mickey   This is just great isn't it. There could be a major health risk here.

Judy   I'll be fine.

Mickey   I was talking about the dog!

Anthony   It's okay, I can get some more from the vet.

Mickey   Make an appointment for Judy while you're there.

Judy   You're not funny.

Mickey   No. *You* took the dog pills. *You're* funny. What the hell's the matter with you? Don't you read labels?

Judy   If you gave me a few Ritalin like you're supposed to, I wouldn't be so damn desperate.

She accidentally rolls off the sofa, landing on the floor.

Mickey   You're not having any Ritalin, not ever. Okay?

She hoists herself onto her hands and knees and starts crawling on all fours towards **Mickey***, growling like a dog.*

Mickey   Now go to bed.

She barks and growls. Pausing only to raise a leg and pee over **Anthony***'s feet. She then heads towards* **Mickey***.*

Mickey   Judy – go to bed. Just – go to bed.

By this point, she is facing **Mickey***'s groin.*

Judy   Not without my bone I won't!

She lunges towards his penis, then collapses with laughter.
Anthony *laughs along with her. But after a moment, he catches* **Mickey***'s glare and stops.*

Anthony   I'll be off, then.

He picks up his bag and edges towards the door.

. . . Judy, please try and just – take it easy. I'll see you in the morning.

She rolls over and he rubs her belly. She wriggles with delight.

Who's a good girl?! I'll come straight here.

Anthony *now heads for the door.*

Judy   Try the park first – I might be having my walk.

Anthony *leaves. She starts laughing to herself, but chokes on the laughter, causing her to cough and retch a little.*

Mickey   If you're gonna throw up, do it in the toilet.

Judy   I prefer the window. If the wind's in the right direction – you can hit the concierge.

She crawls back to the sofa or nearest chair. He pours her a glass of water.

Mickey   Why do you keep doing this to yourself?

Judy   It was an evening out. It just went a bit cock-eyed . . . Is there coffee?

He gives her the water.

Mickey   It's on its way.

Judy   I need a coffee.

He picks up the bits of fruit bowl and pieces of fruit that she earlier hurled across the room. She in the meantime awkwardly drinks some of the water, most of it pouring down her chin.

. . . What are you doing?

Mickey   The fruit bowl hit the wall.

Judy   I missed you? I'm losing my touch. With Luft and Minnelli, my accuracy was deadly.

Mickey   So I hear.

Judy   Sure you hear. Everybody knows about it. They told the world every bad thing about me.

Mickey   From what I see, they told it just as it is.

Judy   If you don't like it – then why don't you go?

Mickey   Maybe I will.

Judy   I don't need you.

Mickey   Right now it sounds a great fucking idea!

Judy   Good. Get the hell out! And take your cheap shit fucking shit-coloured shoes with you.

She grabs almost any object she can get her hands on – beginning with her shoes – and starts throwing everything at him. He crosses to her, grabs her in both his arms and shakes her to a halt.

Mickey   Stop! Stop! For Christ's sake. Is this how it is? You wanna be this?

Judy   I am this!

Mickey   No you're not. This is the drink. Look at yourself. Look!

He pulls her over to a mirror and forces her to look at her self.

Judy   Get your hands off me.

Mickey   That's what the drink and the pills do to you – you see it?

Judy   I see it.

Mickey   Is that what you want?

She pulls herself away from his hold.

Judy   When was it *ever* about what I want!? *I* didn't make this. I was up at 4 a.m., fifteen years old, fourteen hours a day, take this, swallow that. Even my own *mother* insisted I took every pill they gave me. No wonder I skipped down the yellow brick road – I could have *flown* down it!

Mickey   I need some air.

She prevents him from leaving.

Judy   No – you stay and listen. How? – How could I stop? I could barely stand up without those drugs. Let alone sing.

Mickey   Judy –

Judy   When you said you'd marry me, you took on my past – and all that comes with it.

Mickey   I don't accept that.

Judy   You don't have a choice! My God, Mickey, you gotta see the whole picture – it's not this or that, everything just comes at me at once and it crashes from one thing to the other. I can't control it – why can't you see that?

Mickey   I do see it.

Judy   No – no, you don't. (*Snide.*) You're too fucking *young*!

Mickey   Get out of my way.

Judy   I can see how it is for you – (*yelling*) so why can't you see it how it is for *me*!

In her agony, she reaches out her arms as though desperate for the whole world to embrace her. She slumps to the floor and starts to sob. A moment. Then he resigns the battle and sits. Nothing is said for a while. She crawls over to him and takes his hand, caressing it, kissing it.

Judy   . . . Mickey –

Mickey   What?

Judy   . . . Could I have a little whisky?

Mickey (*pulling his hand away*)   Oh, Jesus!

Judy   No – no – just a tiny drop. With soda. I've got a terrible headache. It's so I can sleep.

Mickey   You won't sleep. You're being treated for mange.

Judy   Please – I'm begging you.

Mickey   No!

Judy   Okay – okay . . . So long as you stay . . .

She cuddles up closer to him.

. . . Remember when we were together that first night at your club. Remember how beautiful that was? We talked for

hours . . . We talked through breakfast . . . That's what it will
be like, Mickey. Oh, I know I have bad days. Bad nights.
And we may need to buy the odd fruit bowl . . . But there'll
be more good than bad. I promise you that.

*She takes hold of a nearby cushion and lays down on the floor,
exhausted.*

Mickey   . . . You want a bath or a shower?

Judy (*not listening*)   I'll try harder . . . Don't give up on me.
– I love you, Mickey. You do know that, don't you?

*Realising he won't get an answer, he exits into the bathroom. She
doesn't notice and keeps talking.*

I just need you to know that because – . . . they tend not to
stay around. The men I love. They go while I'm not even
looking. I don't mean it to happen . . . I won't lose you, will
I, Mickey?

He returns from the bathroom. She looks up at him with sad eyes.

. . . Will I?

Mickey   . . . You want anything?

Judy   . . . I want cigarettes. There are no cigarettes.

*He grabs the room keys and exits. She watches him go, wondering if
he's coming back. She cries out to him.*

Judy   . . . Mickey . . .?!

*Music begins. Lighting change. Transition into song sequence. We
are not in concert here. This is nowhere in particular, a space in her
mind. The first lyrics are half-spoken, half-sung as she eases
gradually into the song.*

SONG
'THE MAN THAT GOT AWAY'

*The song ends. She exits slowly to the bathroom as lights fade to
blackout.*

Act Two

Scene One

Lights rise on **Judy** *sat at her dressing-room table in the hotel room. She is without make-up and draped in her dressing gown.* **Anthony** *enters.*

Anthony   I've come from the theatre.

Judy   I'm not there.

Anthony   So I realised. And where's Mickey?

Judy   He has a meeting with Delfont. To discuss a problem.

Anthony   And they didn't invite you?

Judy   I *am* the fucking problem . . .!

Anthony   . . .What time's your car?

Judy   Eleven. I'll walk straight on.

Anthony   But you haven't done your make-up?

Judy   I was just getting around to it. I could have put on some foundation, but – I forgot to bring my bucket and shovel.

He smiles.

Anthony   Would you like some help?

Judy   No.

Anthony   I'll take that as a 'Yes'.

He starts preparing all the make-up.

Judy   You'll take 'No' as a 'Yes'? – How does that work?

Anthony   I'm very good at doing make-up. I used to do it for my mother at the weekends . . . And *still* she was surprised I turned out homosexual . . . Now – let's sort ourselves out here.

He manoeuvres her chair to distance it from the mirror. Then he picks up the stool from elsewhere in the room and places it between her and the dressing table, so that he is facing her.

Okay then – I want you to just look straight ahead and don't move a muscle.

Judy   That's what Minnelli used to say before we had sex.

Anthony (*chuckling*)   At least you were *having* sex. The rest of us are not in such demand. But then again, I suppose you've had enough for both of us.

Judy   That's because I'm so very good at it.

Anthony   So I've heard.

Judy   God, yes. I'm an animal in the bedroom. There's just nothing I won't do.

Anthony   Believe me – your reputation precedes you.

Judy   It does? . . . Is that a good thing?

Anthony   Not if you were planning a *white* wedding.

He takes up a make-up sponge and applies some foundation to it. He waits for her to close her eyes.

. . . Judy, I can't do this unless we have our eyes closed.

Judy   He used to say *that* before we had sex too!

Anthony   . . . I'm waiting.

She shuts her eyes and he applies the foundation to her face.

As he does so, they continue to talk.

We could do this every night, if you wanted. Meet an hour before the show and I could – help make you beautiful.

Judy   You can do that in an hour?

Anthony   Don't you believe in miracles?

Judy   No. Only gravity . . . My chin and tits are in a race to my knees.

He looks horrified by this comment. He re-gathers himself.

Anthony   . . . Let's talk about 'nice' things, shall we? You know – flowers, trees . . . the ballet.

Judy   Men in tights?

Anthony   Precisely. A thing of beauty we can both appreciate. Did you ever meet Nureyev?

Judy   Darling, I've met everybody. Or to be correct – everybody's met me.

Anthony   They have ballet at the Coliseum. I'm very well acquainted with the chap who runs the cloakroom. I'm sure he could steal us a couple of tickets for your night off.

Judy (*heavily sarcastic*)   I have a night off?! Jesus – surely that's some kind of mistake?

Anthony   Mr Delfont's generosity is boundless . . . Now – eye shadow. Which do you want to use?

Judy   Something to bring out the colour of my eyes.

He examines the palette of colours.

Anthony   . . .You don't seem to have it in 'bloodshot' . . .!

Judy   Oh, be nice to me.

Anthony   I'm only teasing. By the time I'm finished, you'll hardly recognise yourself.

Judy   That's nothing new. I was looking in the mirror just now and – it wasn't me looking back. I had no idea who it was at all, at first . . . And then I realised – it was my mother. After all those years of trying to wipe her face from my memory – there she is. In every line and every crack. I knew she'd catch up with me some day.

Anthony   If only you saw what I see.

Judy   Which is?

He applies the eye shadow.

Anthony   Esther from *Meet Me in St Louis* . . . Vicky Lester from *A Star is Born* . . . Dorothy . . .

Judy   . . . And the giant squid from *20,000 Leagues Under the Sea*!

Anthony   You're beautiful. To me and everyone that's ever watched you. So remember that when you next look in the mirror . . . Open your eyes.

He moves out of the way, so that she can fully see her reflection.

. . . I think we're making progress.

Judy   You do?

Anthony   Just wait till I've finished with you.

Judy   Oh – can we wait a little while? I don't want to be ready yet. I like it when I'm not ready. When there's still time to change my mind.

Anthony   I wish you didn't get so nervous.

Judy   It's not nerves, Anthony. It's blind panic.

Anthony   It's not like it's the first time.

Judy   No. But that makes it harder. It was so much easier at the beginning. It's a terrible thing to know what you're capable of . . . And to never get there . . .

He takes hold of her hands.

Anthony   Even at your worst, you wipe the floor with everybody else.

She looks at her hand, noticing it is shaking with nerves.

Judy   . . . Oh God . . . I'm shaking.

Anthony   It'll pass.

Judy   Anthony, I – the medley – I don't know if – if I can remember the words . . . I just –

Anthony   It's alright. You'll be fine.

She looks like she is about to cry.

Don't you dare ruin that make-up. I'll never forgive you.

He gives her a tissue to wipe her eyes. Then he goes to apply lipstick. But she stops his hand by grabbing his wrist.

Judy   I'm frightened.

Anthony   We're all frightened. We go through life like little children. Every single one of us *pretending* to be an adult . . . All you can really do – is find someone to be with who's less scared than you are.

Judy   . . . Someone like Mickey.

Anthony   Well . . . someone . . . Lips.

He applies lipstick to her lips.

There – phase one completed.

He reaches forward and kisses her on the cheek. A moment. Then he kisses her on the lips. This kiss becomes prolonged, lasting longer than either of them expected. After it, they say nothing for a moment.

Judy   . . . You'll need to hold my hand tonight.

Anthony   But how am I supposed to play the piano?

Judy   You know what I mean.

He nods that he does.

Anthony   . . . Now is there anything else I can do for you?

Judy   How about a one-way ticket out of here?

Anthony   Apart from that.

Judy   Well . . . you could help me with my scarf . . .?

Anthony   . . . Certainly, Miss Garland.

He produces her scarf with a flourish and wraps it around her neck.

Judy   Thank you.

Anthony   No, no. Thank *you*.

Judy   For what?

Anthony   . . . For saving my life . . .

Music begins. The band is revealed. A brief blackout while she puts on her jacket and takes up the microphone. Transition into a concert sequence –

Scene Two

SONG
'WHEN YOU'RE SMILING'

Judy *sings the song initially deadpan, without any hint of a smile.*

After singing part of the song, she realises she has got herself tangled in the microphone lead.

Judy (*spoken*)   This thing is attacking me, I feel like I've been lasoo'd.

She sings more of the song, then breaks from it –

(*Spoken.*) I'd like to take a moment to thank you all for coming here tonight . . . and for that matter, I'd like to thank myself for getting here tonight! I tell ya, I've been having a hell of a time.

She sings more of the song, relaxing now and breaking into a smile. But then she becomes suddenly frozen, as though momentarily lost. She looks at **Anthony**.

Anthony (*whispered*)   It's you.

She forces herself back on track and concludes the song. Applause.

Judy   Thank you, Thank you. Let me just get this lead sorted out.

She fiddles with the lead again, then forgets what she was saying.

. . . Now what was I saying Anthony?

Anthony   You were thanking the audience.

Judy   . . . I was? Well, there you go, folks. (*She laughs.*) . . .
– Thank you. This is for you –

He plays a brief introduction to the song 'Dancing in the Dark' on the piano.

Judy   'Blue Skies'.

She gets ready to sing. He suddenly stops, playing nothing.

Judy   . . . Wait, I think someone shot the pianist.

She crosses to him at the piano.

Anthony (*embarassed*)   I don't have that, we don't have it.

Judy   'Blue Skies'.

Anthony   I . . . we don't have it.

Judy   You lost it?

Anthony   No, I –

Judy   Well, we have to sing something, honey, or they'll go and see *The Mousetrap* instead – and I wouldn't wish that on anybody . . . So – ?

Anthony   'Dancing in the Dark'.

Judy   We'll give it a try.

He plays the intro to 'Dancing in the Dark', but she sings the opening lyrics of 'Blue Skies'. When she realises, she stops and storms upstage.

Judy (*spoken, irritated*)   Wait a second, wait a second!

Anthony   I'm sorry, I –

Judy   What exactly is happening here? Either we're under a blue sky or we're in the dark, which is it?

Anthony   I thought we were doing 'Dancing in the Dark' –

Judy (*to the audience*)   I'm sorry, ladies and gentlemen, there's confusion over what time it is and what weather we're having! – Shall we try again?

Anthony   Okay, I'll busk it.

He plays the 'Blue Skies' intro, but she is distracted by the microphone lead again.

Judy   I've got this damn lead round my leg again. It's like a dog on heat, this thing.

Anthony   . . . Judy!

She now starts to sing 'Dancing in the Dark' until she realises the whole thing is now getting really screwed up.

Judy (*a yell*)   Christ! (*Stopping* **Anthony**.) Okay – okay . . . It's not my night, is it! – Look, I think we'll call it quits and take the interval now.

Anthony   No, Judy, we can't –

She pushes all the sheet music onto the floor.

Judy   Intermission!

On **Anthony**'*s cue, the band plays her exit music, 'Somewhere Over the Rainbow'. She moves downstage to talk to the audience,* **Anthony** *quieting the music as she does so.*

Judy   So you good folks go and get a few drinks and I'll – well, I'll probably do the same – race you to the bar! We're gonna get this God damn lead fixed. So you *fuck off* – and come back when they call you.

She throws the microphone to the floor. It lands with a thump. She storms off. The music rises again to full volume.

Blackout.

Scene Three

The hotel room. **Judy** *storms in. She searches the room for alcohol, yelling 'damn' each time she fails to find anything. Shortly,* **Mickey** *enters and slams the door behind him.*

Mickey   What the hell are you doing!?

Judy   I want a drink.

Mickey   You have to leave and go back in five minutes – five minutes maximum – you hear me?

Judy   I just got here!

Mickey   You can't leave the venue during the show! People saw you hailing a cab. Half of them think you're not going back.

Judy   Maybe they're right.

Mickey   Just take a quick drink or whatever it is you want and let's get back there.

Judy   You've hidden all the damn bottles!

Mickey (*giving in*)   . . . They're in the bathroom.

Judy (*waiting*)   You want *me* to get them?!

He heads into the toilet to retrieve the hidden bottles.

This is just getting crazy, all of it. I have to come back all the way here just to get a damn drink. Those bottles should be in my dressing room. My room is empty. It's like a tomb in there.

Mickey   Your room is full of flowers.

Judy   Exactly – it's like a *tomb* in there . . . ! . . . And I can't drink flowers, Mickey.

He hands over the bottle of whisky. She immediately fetches a glass and pours herself a large drink.

Mickey   What was that all about? You cut the first half short by thirty minutes! They'd hardly sat down.

Judy   I wasn't getting anywhere.

Mickey   Well, there was no need to curse at everyone!

Judy   You think it's easy up there? It's hard enough entertaining these people – you want me to be polite?! I just want life to be a little easier. I've had enough. I've had it, you hear me?

Mickey   You've got three minutes.

Judy   No. No! I'm finished for tonight.

Mickey   Judy – listen to me very carefully. There are hundreds of people in that theatre waiting for you and we need every penny that they've paid out – so you just pull yourself together because you *are* going back.

Judy   I can't do any more tonight. I'm shaking, look at me. I raised my hand in that spotlight and I saw it tremble – tremble – that's when I know – when I'm losing control.

Mickey   Look, let's just go back and –

Judy   Mickey, darling – how much longer do you think you can keep throwing me on there and expecting the best of me. I can't do it anymore, it's too much. Call Delfont and tell him to give the people their money back.

Anthony   Honey – there's a row of people in wheelchairs.

Judy   Well, if they wheeled them in, they can wheel them back out again! . . . Let's wrap the whole thing up and go back to California. I hate this God-forsaken place.

Mickey   You love London.

Judy   I do not. I hate the people and the theatres and all those big red busses – they piss me off.

Mickey   Are you insane?

Judy   Yes! Yes – I am. And all thanks to you for bringing me back to this hell.

Mickey   Oh, stop.

Judy   It's hell!

Mickey   Have another drink.

Judy   You're *encouraging* me to drink?

Mickey   Whatever it takes.

Anthony *enters.*

Anthony   What are you doing here?

Judy   Having a drink.

Anthony *looks at his watch.*

Mickey   It's okay, we'll be heading back in two minutes.

Judy   We will *not* be heading back.

Mickey   Anthony, please – you talk to her.

Judy   I don't want to talk to him.

Anthony   It wasn't my fault, I was just playing what –

Mickey   Anthony, calm down – have a drink.

Anthony   I never drink during a show!

Judy   Bully for you.

Anthony   Are we going back?

Judy   No we are not.

Mickey   Yes, we are!

She slams her glass down.

Judy   I said no! I sing if and when I want to. And you are not getting me back on that stage tonight – or any other night.

Mickey   You can't afford to cancel the show. Pull out of this deal and you'll –

Judy   Screw the money! I'll live without it.

Mickey   And spend the rest of your life in court. You've got too many debts.

Judy (*in disbelief*)   How can I have? I've been screaming my lungs out there for weeks.

Mickey   That does not wipe out ten years. There's a list of staff demanding back pay that is unbelievable. You had every queer from here to San Francisco on your pay role.

Judy   I needed them!

Mickey   Well you don't need them any more.

Judy   Why not?

Mickey   Because I can handle all that.

Judy   Oh sure you can. I look like a car wreck for Christ's sake! You're obviously not handling it very fucking well.

Mickey   Well, maybe that's because *you* are such a fuck-up.

Anthony   For heaven's sake, do you have to swear all the time?!

Judy/Mickey (*in unison*)   Fuck off!

Anthony   . . . Fine. I don't need to listen to this. I'll come back in two minutes to see if you're done.

He leaves the room.

Judy   . . . This whole thing is a mess. I shouldn't have listened to any of you. Six weeks in that damn hole. Didn't they tell anyone here that vaudeville died a dozen years ago? Why is it *my* responsibility to bring it back from the dead? For God's sake, we all got dragged through the funeral, so leave it at that. Let's just take the first ship out of here.

Mickey   No. We finish the run.

Judy   What the hell is this obsession with finishing things? Shows close, it happens.

Mickey   It's not just a show. This is everything.

Judy   We don't need it. Listen to me – (*He resists.*) Listen – listen –

She cups his face in her hands, pleading.

We have each other. We'll get married and buy a small house somewhere. A small house, somewhere quiet. And rest. You can hold me in your arms – and we won't tell anybody where we are. It'll be just the two of us. We could bury her, Mickey. We could put Judy Garland deep into the ground and never see her again.

Mickey   We just can't kill her. Everybody loves her.

Judy   I don't want to be loved up there. I want to be loved down here.

Mickey   You are. For God's sake, we're getting married.

Judy   But who are you marrying, Mickey? Me or her?

Mickey (*Grabbing her and looking into her eyes*) I gave up *everything* for you!

Judy   I'm sorry.

Mickey   No, no – I'm not. You're the greatest thing that ever happened in my shitty life. I love you. (*They embrace.*) It's all going to be ok . . . I'll make sure of that. (*A pause.*) . . . Now – do you trust me?

Judy   . . . Yes.

Mickey   I mean, really trust me?

Judy   I do.

Mickey   . . . Well then . . . We have to go back. And finish the show.

Judy   But . . .

Mickey   Judy – you have to.

Judy   . . . No, Mickey – no, no.

Mickey Judy!

Judy No – I'm *begging* you! I am all *sung out* . . . I'm sorry, my angel. (*Strong.*) I just can't do it.

She breaks away from him. He is infuriated. He paces around the room, tormented by the situation. Then he stops and looks at her.

Mickey . . . Alright . . . Tell me what you – . . . Judy. (*She looks at him.*) . . . Tell me what you want, I'll get it for you.

Judy . . . What?

Mickey . . . You can take whatever you want, so long as it gets you back up there – What do you need? . . . Ritalin?

Judy You've spent the last month getting me off them.

Mickey Yes, but . . . (*A beat.*) . . . You *have* to finish the show. So – how many?

Judy You've got some?

He goes to locate the pills which are well hidden elsewhere in the room. Her attitude changes immediately and she gets hungry for the pills. She crosses to him, her hand out ready.

Judy Well, I – (*She stares at the bottle.*)

Mickey You finish the programme from the first half and then go straight into the second set. We still have to give them the full show, okay?

Judy . . . Okay . . . You'll have to let me go to my dressing room when we get there. In 15 minutes, I'm gonna want a piss . . . And I don't want to do it half-way through 'Ol' Man River'.

Mickey Fine.

He empties some pills into his hand and counts out half a dozen. He pauses before giving them to her, uncertain again. Unable to wait, she grabs the pills out of his hands. And swallows a couple of them dry. As she does so, **Anthony** *walks into the room.*

Anthony   So? (*He sees* **Mickey** *and* **Judy** *with the pills.*) – What are you doing? Mickey – what the hell are you – ?! What are they?

She fetches herself a drink and swallows the rest of the tablets, one at a time.

Mickey   I know what I'm doing.

Anthony   No, Mickey.

Mickey   Look, there's no choice here – I'm resolving the situation.

Anthony   Oh, well that's real genius. This is the great plan, is it? Drugs to make her sing, make her dance – then a few more to get her down the aisle.

He crosses to her.

Don't drink as well.

He takes the glass from her and puts it down.

Anthony   This is insanity. Why don't we just cancel?

Mickey   Because she needs this show.

Anthony   You mean *you* need it. This is your meal ticket. You're here for every penny you can get.

Mickey   You don't understand this.

Anthony   Oh, don't I? (*Heavy sarcasm.*) When's your book coming out?

Mickey   Will you give your mouth a rest. You have no idea how deep in the ditch she is. She's got nothing! I'm all she has.

Anthony   And I thought less than nothing wasn't possible.

Mickey   *Somebody* has to help her. You guys – you *fags* – you just stand back and watch!

Anthony   Oh, don't be –

Mickey   What the hell is it with you people? The more she falls apart, the more you adore her.

Anthony   That is not true, we –

Mickey   It *is* true. You love all the misery. If she was found half dead in a gutter, you'd all come in your pants.

Anthony   Don't you dare – you have no right! *We* have given her everything. Shown her the kind of loyalty and devotion you couldn't even dream of.

Mickey   She doesn't need 'devotion' you idiot. She needs someone to rescue her. When I met her she was a fucking mess. I'm the guy that put her back up there.

Anthony   And you think that's what she wants?

Mickey   I know it is.

Anthony   You don't know anything. You're not remotely what she needs.

Mickey   And I suppose you are?

Anthony   Yes. Because we've always been there for her. And we'll be there long after you've gone.

Mickey   I got bad news for you. I'm not going anywhere.

Anthony (*turning to her*)   Judy – we do *not* have to go back. What do *you* want to do?

She looks at **Mickey**. *He nods at her.*

Judy   . . . I'm ready.

Anthony   Let me just say that after what you've taken . . . If it goes wrong – I can't bail you out. You'll be on your own up there.

Judy   I'm *always* on my own up there . . .

Fade to blackout. Background noise of a band warming up and audience bustle.

Scene Four

Lights rise on a back stage area at the Talk of the Town venue. It is lit only by a small shaft of light. Enter the **ASM**, *all in black. He is slightly, subtly camp, carries a walkie-talkie and looks panicked.*

ASM I'm looking, Brian, I'm looking!

He crosses the stage and exits. **Mickey** *appears, smoking a cigarette. Then* **Judy** *comes in from the opposite side. Her speech is slightly slurred and her eyes glazed over, but a volcano of nervous energy bubbles underneath.*

Mickey You take a piss?

Judy Yes, but don't ask me where . . . Is the house still full?

Mickey Yes, they're still waiting for you. You're the only one they'd wait for, Judy. (*He holds her.*) Because you're wonderful.

Judy Oh. Thank you, darling.

Anthony *enters.*

Mickey I'll be out the front. I'll be there with you every single moment. Okay?

Judy Yes.

Mickey I love you.

He kisses her on the lips, in clear view of **Anthony**.

Judy I love you too.

Mickey I know you do.

He looks across to **Anthony**, *then walks away. As he does so, the* **ASM** *enters.*

ASM Oh my goodness – Miss Garland! (*Talking into a walkie-talkie.*) I've found her. She's stage left. (*To* **Judy**.) Are you going straight on?

Anthony Just – give us a moment more.

The **ASM** *looks at his stopwatch.*

ASM   No, Mr Chapman, you really need to go straight on.

Anthony (*insistent*)   A moment – please.

The **ASM** *just stands there, waiting.*

Judy (*drily*)   Can we get you a chair!?

The **ASM** *takes the hint and leaves.*

Judy   . . . He's weird. I think he escaped from somewhere.

Anthony   . . . How many did he give you?

Judy   Huh?

Anthony   How many *pills* did Mickey give you?

Judy   Pills? Darling, I haven't taken any pills. No, I'm just full of 'go' tonight, I'm on a roll. I just wanna get back out there. They are a terrific audience tonight. Aren't they? And forgiving. Don't you think?

Anthony   I don't know.

Judy   You don't know? Well, you should turn around and look sometimes. There are *people* sitting out there.

She coughs.

. . . Is there any water here, I'm very dry.

Anthony   Wasn't there any in your room?

Judy   Oh I couldn't find it.

Anthony   Should have been on the table.

Judy   No, the *room* – I couldn't find the *room*! All I found was the fire bucket. This place is a maze. I met Harry Houdini still trying to get out.

Anthony   Judy –

Judy   What?

Anthony   I'm not going out there.

Judy   You gotta! Who else is gonna play?

Anthony   I know, I know, I just –

Judy   Darling, I love that you care. But you should never let personal things affect your work. That's unprofessional. – Now – you get out there and start playing.

We start hearing the audience doing a slow hand-clap.

Anthony   No. If this is the only way I can protect you – no.

Judy   I don't need protecting – not out there.

*The **ASM** appears again, stopwatch in hand.*

Anthony (*referring to the audience*)   Listen to them.

Judy   . . . Fuck 'em. I'll get 'em back. They don't scare me. This is *my* house. You come and play for me – okay?

Anthony   I don't think I can.

Judy   Listen to me, Anthony –

She takes his hand.

Are you listening to me?

Anthony   Yes.

Judy   When we go on stage, that's – that's *our* time together. You and me. It's just us. You know . . . The plain truth is that . . . I need you, my darling. I always have. Not just at the piano – no, no, I mean – I need you . . . in my life . . . Am I making sense? (*To the **ASM**.*) Am I making . . . What the hell am I asking you for? (*Back to **Anthony**.*) . . . Come on – let's go. Let's go – *together* – and finish the show. We *have* to finish the show.

*She then gives a signal to the **ASM**.*

ASM (*into the walkie talkie as he exits*)   Thirty seconds, she's ready.

*The drumming that marks the beginning of the coming song now begins. **Judy** immediately moves to her position on the Talk of the Town stage.*

Music begins. Lighting change.

Transition into concert sequence – with **Judy** *drugged and dangerous, a performance on the edge.*

SONG
'COME RAIN OR COME SHINE'

At the end of the song – blackout.

Scene Five

Lights rise on the hotel room. **Judy** *is asleep on the settee, covered in a variety of bed sheets.* **Mickey** *is at the piano, tinkering at the keys, playing a few notes of gentle improvised jazz music. She begins to wake.*

Judy   Oh god . . . oh God . . .

Mickey   Judy?

Judy   I'm gonna chuck up.

Mickey   Do you need the bathroom?

Judy   I feel terrible . . . Argh!

She suddenly feels a sharp pain in her stomach, bends double in agony.

Mickey   It's alright, it'll pass.

Judy   I feel terrible . . . Really terrible.

Mickey   I'll get you some pills, they'll perk you up.

Judy   My throat's so dry – I need a drink.

He fetches her a glass of water.

Mickey   You sure you don't need the bathroom?

Judy   I've never been this bad, never. My head is screaming.

Mickey   Give it half an hour.

Judy   . . . Did we finish the show?

Mickey   Yes. They loved you.

Judy   . . . How many did I take?

Mickey   . . . I wasn't counting.

She looks over at him, frightened for a moment. He counts out three tablets from one of the bottles.

Mickey   Take a few of these. They'll fix you up.

Judy   No. I don't want them.

Mickey   You will.

Judy   I'll just rest.

Mickey   Okay. I'll leave them here.

He deposits the pill bottle in her clear view and close to hand. Again, she reacts to a sharp pain in her stomach.

Mickey   Just breathe, breathe . . . It'll pass . . . You should take these now. Come on . . .

He helps raise her to a sitting position and then forcibly feeds **Judy** *with the pills.*

Judy   . . . Don't lose track of these things. Too many can kill you, you know.

Mickey   I know.

He makes her drink some water.

Judy   You're clear on that, right? It can give you a seizure, you can –

Mickey   I know.

Judy   . . . Oh God. I didn't ever want you to see me like this.

Mickey   That's okay. I knew what I was buying into.

Judy   . . . And still you want to stay?

Mickey   Of course I do.

Judy   They all go eventually. Once they realise I'm just a frail old lady.

Mickey   Not me.

Judy   That's what drove Sid away. The sadness . . . Oh God – my head . . . Honey – could you get me some ice?

There is a knock on the door. He opens it. **Anthony** *is standing there.*

Mickey   She doesn't want to see you.

Anthony   I'm just checking that she's alright.

Mickey   She's fine.

Anthony   Are you sure?

Mickey   I'm sure. Goodbye.

He is just closing the door on him when she calls out.

Judy   Is that Anthony? Anthony!

Mickey *opens the door again, reluctantly.*

Anthony   Yes, it's me.

She holds her hand out towards him and **Anthony** *enters the room. He embraces her.* **Mickey** *stares at them for a moment, then finds a reason to go.*

Mickey   . . . I'll get the ice.

Mickey *leaves the room, closing the door behind him.*

Judy   Anthony –

Anthony   Yes.

Judy   I want you to help me with something.

Anthony   Anything.

Judy   I need to get over to the window – help me up.

He helps her to her feet.

Now stay there. Don't move.

She crosses to the window.

Anthony   What are you doing?

She proceeds to throw the pills out of the window, a few at a time.

Judy   . . . Feeding the pigeons. Take a look in half an hour – half will be doing cartwheels – and the rest in a coma.

She makes herself laugh, but the laughter becomes tears and pain.

. . . I'm never taking these again. Not ever. (*She turns to him.*) Does that make you happy?

Anthony   More than you realise.

He goes over to the window and sits on the ledge beside her.

Judy   You were told to stay there.

Anthony   Oh, since when have I ever listened to you? . . . I think you should phone and cancel the shows right now.

Judy   Oh, I – I don't think I can. Mickey doesn't want me to.

Anthony   Never mind what Mickey wants.

Judy   . . . It's only a few more shows. And then . . . we'll settle into a little house, and have a most wonderful marriage.

His head drops.

. . . You don't approve . . .?

Anthony   Of course I don't.

Judy   Oh, he's not so bad. He's my protector. He's young and he's handsome – and he loves me. It's a miracle.

Anthony   That's one word for it.

Judy   You'll see. We're going to have a wonderful wedding – here in London. In Chelsea. You'll come along.

Anthony   No, I won't.

Judy   Yes, you will. I'll let you be bridesmaid. And we'll have a reception at Quaglino's. It will be full of stars – Bette Davis, Veronica Lake, Lana Turner, Ginger Rogers –

Anthony   None of them will come.

Judy   What?

Anthony   None of them will be there, Judy. They don't want to see you making a fool of yourself.

She slaps his face – and breaks away from him. She heads back to the sofa.

Judy   You should be happy for me!

Anthony   Why? When he's not remotely right for you in any way. He'll never give you what you need.

Judy   Which is?

Anthony   Love. Unconditional love.

He approaches her.

. . . Which is what *I'm* offering you.

Judy   You?

He sits next to her on the sofa.

Anthony   . . . I'll care for you. You'll never do anything you don't want to. You'll come and live with me . . . I'm not wealthy, but – I have enough. I can give piano lessons and I have money put away for a rainy day. And in Brighton, we get lots of those . . . But it doesn't matter, because we can sit inside. There's a big bay window, and it's so beautiful – you can watch the waves crashing in as the rain drums on the roof and – it's warm . . . and comfortable . . . just sitting there looking out at the world.

Judy   . . . Don't you get bored?

Anthony   Yes! It's wonderful. We'd fill the day with nothing. We'd cook food and read trashy magazines and go for walks.

Judy   Oh, I don't walk – people follow me.

Anthony   But you'll be happy. So people won't recognise you.

Judy   If I'm on a pier in the rain, they fucking well better.

Anthony   . . . You'll never reach for pills or drown yourself in whisky. You'll never need to sing . . . Well – maybe just for good friends late at night. And I'll spend every hour of every day looking after you.

Judy   It sounds . . . Well, it –

Anthony   I'm a wonderful cook. Do you like shepherd's pie?

Judy   I love shepherd's pie. And what's that thing with the frogs and the sausages – ?

Anthony   . . . Oh – toad in the hole. I can do that.

Judy   Will you show me?

Anthony   Yes.

Judy   I'd love you to show me. I've hardly ever cooked, it takes too long – there are TV shows to record . . .

Anthony   Sometimes I cook the whole day. Make a feast.

Judy   But all that clearing up. When I made pancakes once, it was like armageddon in there.

Anthony   It doesn't matter, we can have a maid.

Judy   Can we?

Anthony   Yes, we can afford that. She can come in while we're asleep.

Judy   In the same . . . Would we sleep in the same . . .?

Anthony   I haven't really thought about that.

Judy   No, I don't suppose you have.

Anthony   Well . . . there – won't be many fireworks in
that department. But you won't miss it. You'll be too happy
to notice.

Judy   Do you think?

Anthony   . . . Well, if you're desperate, I'm sure we could
find someone at the end of the pier.

He takes both her hands and looks earnestly into her eyes.

. . . Listen . . . Don't marry Mickey. Don't marry that *awful*
man. Come away with me. Let me look after you . . . Let me
love you . . .

Nothing happens for a moment. Then, the door opens and **Mickey**
*comes back into the room, carrying a small bucket of ice. He looks at
both of them.*

Mickey   What's going on? . . . Judy?

Judy (*after a moment*)   Nothing . . . Nothing – we were just
. . . Anthony and I – (*Full of sorrow, but resolute.*) we were just
saying 'goodbye'.

She turns away from **Anthony**, *fighting back the tears. He is
devastated. After a moment, he gets up and moves to the door, and
exits.*

Mickey   . . . How are you feeling?

Judy   Oh . . . God knows . . .

Mickey   We should think about something to eat. You need
to be getting ready. You've got a show in five hours.

Judy   Do you think they're still expecting me?

Mickey   Of course. They hate it when you fall down,
but they love watching you get back up again. That's what
you do.

Judy   That's who I am . . .

Mickey (*seeing her sadness*)   Hey, don't look so . . . It's
nearly over.

She looks at him and nods, forces a smile.

Mickey   . . . It's all for you, Judy. You know that, right? It's only ever been for you.

Judy   . . . I'm cold.

Mickey   You're in England – what did you expect? – I'll find a blanket.

He heads towards the bedroom.

Judy   No – just . . .

He stops, realising she just wants to be held in his arms. He does this, embracing her warmly.

Mickey   Better?

Judy   Better.

He kisses her forehead.

Mickey   . . . I think a few changes would be a good thing. I guess to start we need a new piano player?

Judy   I think perhaps we do.

Mickey   *I* could play for you. How's that for an idea?

Judy   . . . Well, it's an idea . . .

Mickey   Trust me, things will be a lot easier without that guy around.

Judy   I like Anthony.

Mickey   There's a lot of things you like that aren't good for you.

He releases the embrace and gets up.

. . . Why don't you get dressed? Then we can go out and eat somewhere.

Judy   'Somewhere'? Oh I tried that once – I didn't like it.

Mickey (*smiling*)   That's funny.

Judy   Yeah, I'm a regular vaudevillian . . . When I was –

Mickey   (*cutting her off*)   Stop speaking now. Rest your voice. Okay?

He now heads into the bedroom.

Judy   Okay. (*After* **Mickey**'*s exit.*) . . . What else is there to say anyway . . .?

Lights now start gently fading down on the scene. When mid-way to blackout, a spotlight rises on **Anthony** *as he re-enters. The song 'Somewhere Over the Rainbow' begins to play gently in the background, solo piano. It underscores all the dialogue that follows.* **Anthony** *speaks directly to the audience. Though this speech is narrative, it must still be identifiably* **Anthony** *who is speaking, fully in character*

Anthony   Judy married Mickey Deans at Chelsea Registry Office on 15 March 1969 . . . Just three months later, on 22 June, at her home in London – Judy died. She had taken an overdose of sedatives. Seconal capsule barbiturates – ten times the dose. She was forty-seven.

The light fades out on **Judy**.

Anthony   . . . Her New York funeral was paid for by Frank Sinatra, and James Mason delivered the eulogy. The mourners included Cary Grant, Sammy Davis, Jr., Dean Martin and Audrey Hepburn . . . and twenty thousand people filed past the coffin . . . Also present, was the last of her five husbands, Mickey Deans. And, at the back – a small handful of piano players . . . I was just one of them.

The light on **Anthony** *fades down as the* **Radio Interviewer** *appears on stage, dimly lit. A spot rises gently on* **Judy**. *They continue the radio interview from Act One. The piano music continues as underscoring.*

Radio Interviewer   And finally – Judy, you've been singing on stage and film since you were a child. Your entire life. Do you ever think there'll come a time when you'll stop singing?

Judy   Well, you know, I don't really sing for myself. I do it for other people. And the minute the public don't want me to sing – then, that will be the end.

Radio Interviewer   A day, I'm sure, that will never come. And for those unlucky enough not to see Judy Garland at the Talk of the Town, here's a couple of tracks from your wonderful recordings. Each of them a classic, to ensure that you will live for ever.

Judy   Well, you know, immortality would be very nice . . . Yes, I'd like that . . . Immortality might just make up for everything . . .

Blackout on the **Radio Interviewer***, who exits. The spotlight now rises fully on* **Judy***. She begins to sing, with* **Anthony** *(dimly lit in the distance) accompanying her at the piano.*

SONG
'SOMEWHERE OVER THE RAINBOW'

She begins at the lyric 'Some day I'll wish upon a star'.

During the section of the song that is music only (no lyrics), a light rises on **Mickey***, watching her. She looks at him and then at* **Anthony***. Then lights fade out on both men, so that only* **Judy** *is lit. She sings the final part of the song. The play-out music for the song is played by the full band, building to a crescendo. The spotlight closes in tightly on* **Judy***'s face, as the music ends. Blackout.*

Curtain.